Taylor Swift

WILDEST DREAMS

a biography

By Erica Wainer

Illustrated by Joanie Stone

CLARION BOOKS
An Imprint of HarperCollinsPublishers

Taylor Swift spent her childhood
running barefoot in Pennsylvania . . .

. . . inventing fairy-tale worlds,
baking cookies,
and creating magical memories
at her family's Christmas tree farm.

There, Taylor rode horses.

She helped ready the trees.

She listened to country music sung by

Faith

LeAnn

Shania

Dolly

Patsy

the Chicks

her grandmother *Marjorie*, too.

But what Taylor loved most of all . . .

. . . was *writing*.

Taylor loved writing and performing songs.

Taylor sang
for strangers at the beach
and at garden club meetings.

At coffee shops
and at open mic nights.

She sang the national anthem in
massive arenas.

For Taylor,
singing and songwriting
felt as necessary
as breathing.

So Taylor and her family—
her mom, dad, and younger brother—
moved to Nashville, Tennessee.

Taylor handed out recordings of her songs
to folks who worked on Music Row.

She didn't take no for an answer.
She learned how to play the guitar.

And then Taylor Swift
became the youngest songwriter
ever signed to her record label.

Taylor sang at the famous Bluebird Cafe in Nashville.
Many talented singers had been discovered there . . .

. . . and now it was Taylor's turn.

Her debut album, full of songs she wrote, was a hit.

Taylor was only sixteen, and this was just the beginning.

Feelings that had always been important to Taylor—

the **enchantment** of first love, friends and **bad blood**, **the best days** with family, the **peace** that comes with being honest, the **exile** of heartbreak, **shaking off** criticism and coming back strong—imbued her music.

She wanted—most of all—to connect with her listeners.

The songs she wrote were her words;
they came from her pens,
and from her *heart*.

Taylor wrote all kinds of songs:

Teardrops on my Guitar

BLANK SPACE

Country

POP

folk

cardigan

She won

award

after award

after award.

As Taylor's popularity grew,
so did her bond with her fans.
Select listeners who followed Taylor online
were invited to secret sessions to hear her albums
before anyone else.

They began to look for hidden Easter-egg messages
in her lyrics and her liner notes.

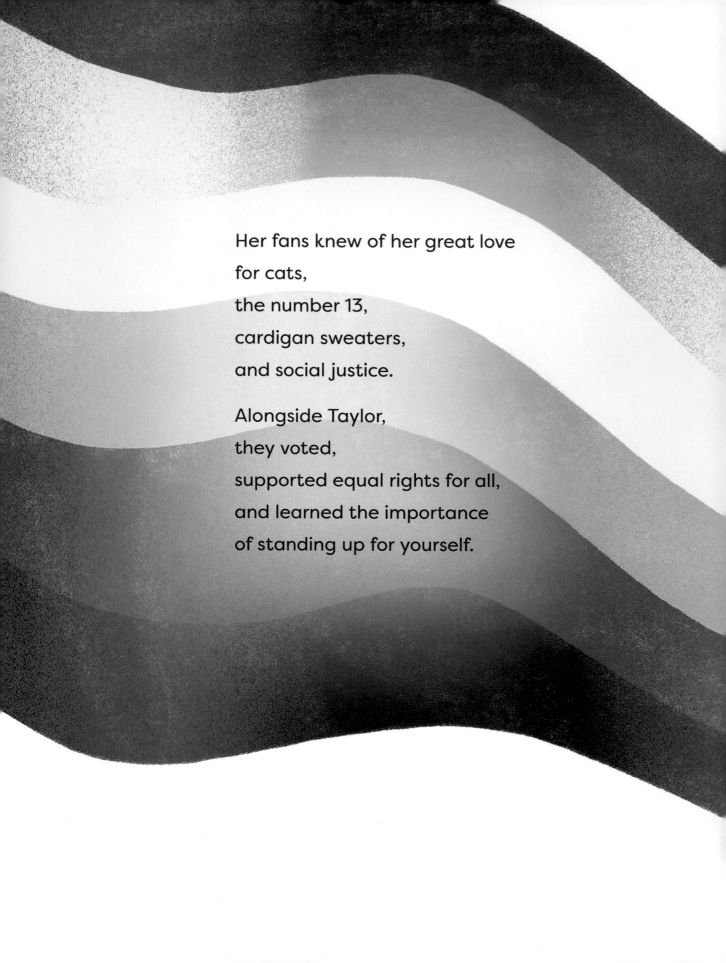

Her fans knew of her great love
for cats,
the number 13,
cardigan sweaters,
and social justice.

Alongside Taylor,
they voted,
supported equal rights for all,
and learned the importance
of standing up for yourself.

Taylor wanted to show people
how she felt about her *words*.
Her early albums no longer belonged to her.

And so she began to record them *all over again*.

Taylor took her albums on a worldwide tour, entertaining millions . . .

. . . and showing everyone what it looks like when a young girl with a *dream* of sharing her words with those around her finds so many people who want to *listen*.

Taylor says her songs are written with three kinds of pens:

glitter

quill

fountain

With these pens, she can . . .
Make *sparks fly*
and ask *questions...*
Chase her *wildest dreams*
and craft the most beautiful *love stories*.

There's no stopping Taylor.

NOTES: The Tortured Poets Department

she has so many

Stories

left to tell ♡

For the loves of my life—Chris, Claire, and Ian —E. W.

For the Swifties —J. S.

Taylor Swift: Wildest Dreams
Copyright © 2024 by HarperCollins Publishers
All rights reserved. Manufactured in Italy. No part of this book may be
used or reproduced in any manner whatsoever without written permission
except in the case of brief quotations embodied in critical articles and reviews.
For information address HarperCollins Children's Books, a division of
HarperCollins Publishers, 195 Broadway, New York, NY 10007.
www.harpercollinschildrens.com

Library of Congress Control Number: 2024937851
ISBN 978-0-06-339917-4

The artist used Photoshop to create the digital illustrations for this book.
Typography and lettering by Molly Fehr
24 25 26 27 28 RTLO 10 9 8 7 6 5 4 3 2 1
First Edition

Sources

Bried, E. "Taylor Swift Has 1,056,375 Friends." *Self*, March 2009.

Chilton, M. "How Taylor Swift's Debut Album Set Her Apart from the Rest."
uDiscover Music, October 24, 2023, www.udiscovermusic.com/stories
/taylor-swift-debut-album.

Cutter, K. "Taylor Made." *Marie Claire*, July 2010.

Grigoriadis, V. "The Very Pink, Very Perfect Life of Taylor Swift." *Rolling Stone*,
March 5, 2009.

Raab, S. "The ESQ&A: Taylor Swift." *Esquire*, November 2014.

Rahman, A. "Taylor Swift Reveals Her Writing Process in Nashville Songwriter
Awards Speech." *Hollywood Reporter*, September 21, 2022, www.hollywood
reporter.com/news/music-news/taylor-swift-songwriting-process-nashville-
speech-1235224700.

Rys, R. "Exit Interview: Taylor Swift." *Philadelphia Magazine*, October 21, 2008,
www.phillymag.com/news/2008/10/21/exit-interview-taylor-swift.

Waterman, L. "Swift Ascent." *Teen Vogue*, March 2009.